Joan of Arc

Brave Soldier for Peace

1412–1431
Born in Domrémy, France
Feast Day: May 30
Community Role: Soldier

Text by Barbara Yoffie
Illustrated by Jeff Albrecht

Liguori
ONE LIGUORI DRIVE
LIGUORI MO 63057-9999

Dedication

To my family:
my parents Jim and Peg,
my husband Bill,
our son Sam and daughter-in-law Erin,
and our precious grandchildren
Ben, Lucas, and Andrew

To all the children I have had the privilege of
teaching throughout the years.

Imprimi Potest:
Stephen T. Rehrauer, CSsR, Provincial
Denver Province, The Redemptorists

Published by Liguori Publications
Liguori, Missouri 63057

To order, visit Liguori.org or call 800-325-9521.

p ISBN 978-0-7648-2554-5
e ISBN 978-0-7648-7005-7

Liguori Publications, a nonprofit corporation, is an apostolate of The
Redemptorists. To learn more about The Redemptorists, visit Redemptorists.com.

Printed in the United States of America
19 18 17 16 15 / 5 4 3 2 1
First Edition

Dear Parents and Teachers:

Saints and Me! is a series of children's books about saints, with six books in each set. The first set, *Saints of North America,* honors holy men and women who blessed and served the land we call home. The second set, *Saints of Christmas,* includes heavenly heroes who inspire us through Advent and Christmas and teach us to love the Infant Jesus. The third set, *Saints for Families,* introduces saints who modeled God's love within and for the domestic Church.

Saints for Communities explores six individuals from different times and places who served Jesus through their various roles and professions. Saint John Baptist de la Salle taught children and founded a familiar educational system. Saint Joan of Arc helped to bring peace to the country of France. The Apostle Matthew was a tax collector before deciding to follow Jesus. The Apostle Thomas preached and built churches. Saint Cecilia sang hymns to Jesus in her heart. And Michael the Archangel is well-known for his protection.

Which saint doubted Jesus' resurrection? Which one fought a heavenly battle? Which saint heard heavenly voices? Who sold everything he owned? Which saint was first named Levi? Which saint was married against her will? Find out in the *Saints for Communities* set—part of the *Saints and Me!* series—and help your child connect to the lives of the saints.

Introduce your children or students to the *Saints and Me!* series as they:

—**READ** about the lives of the saints and are inspired by their stories.

—**PRAY** to the saints for their intercession.

—**CELEBRATE** the saints and relate them to their lives.

saints of communities

 John Baptist
Teacher

 Joan of Arc
Soldier

 Matthew
Banker

 Thomas
Construction worker

 Cecilia
Musician

 Michael
Police officer

Joan of Arc was a brave and holy girl. She lived in France at a time when there were kings, castles, soldiers, and wars. French soldiers fought English soldiers. Joan wanted peace, not war. God made her a hero and a saint.

Joan lived in the small town of Domrémy. Everyone knew her because she was so nice. Joan liked to go to church and pray. She took care of the animals on her family's farm and spent time in her father's garden. Whenever she could, Joan helped her neighbors and did kind deeds.

One summer day, as Joan walked in the garden, she heard someone call her name. She looked around but did not see anyone. A voice said, "You must help France and the king. God wants you to send the English army away!" Joan tried not to listen to the voices.

"I'm too young. I do not know how to fight," Joan thought to herself. But she thought about what the voices said and prayed. She knew God was speaking to her.

Finally Joan went to see the French commander of the army. "I am here to help France win the war," she said. The commander laughed at her! "Go home. Do not bother me," he said loudly. But Joan knew what to do. She had to see the future king of France. His name was Charles.

Joan went to the king's castle. There were lots of people there. She walked over to Charles and said boldly, "God sent me to help you. We will go to the cathedral in Reims, and you will be crowned king!" Charles did not believe Joan. He sent her to talk to some holy men. After asking her many questions they said, "Joan is a good Christian. You can trust her."

Joan led the French soldiers to the city of Orleans. To prepare for battle, she cut her hair and dressed in men's clothes. She wore armor and carried a banner with the words *"Jesus, Mary."* The people smiled and waved as she rode by on her horse. Joan told the soldiers, "Fight hard! Do your best."

The French army fought the English army and won the battle at Orleans. There were many other battles. Joan and the army fought very hard and won again and again! People cheered for them. Finally the English armies started to leave France.

Now the road to Reims was safe for travel. Charles went to the cathedral. Joan stood next to Charles when he was crowned king of France. All the people in the cathedral, especially Joan, clapped and cheered, "Hooray for King Charles VII!"

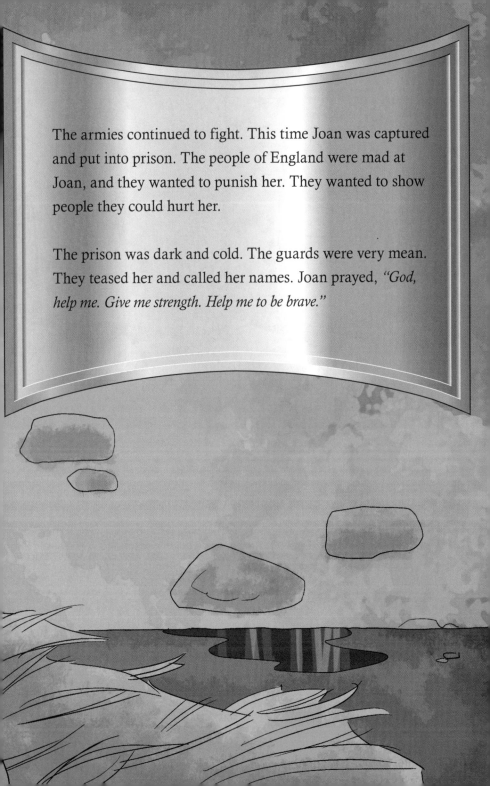

The armies continued to fight. This time Joan was captured and put into prison. The people of England were mad at Joan, and they wanted to punish her. They wanted to show people they could hurt her.

The prison was dark and cold. The guards were very mean. They teased her and called her names. Joan prayed, *"God, help me. Give me strength. Help me to be brave."*

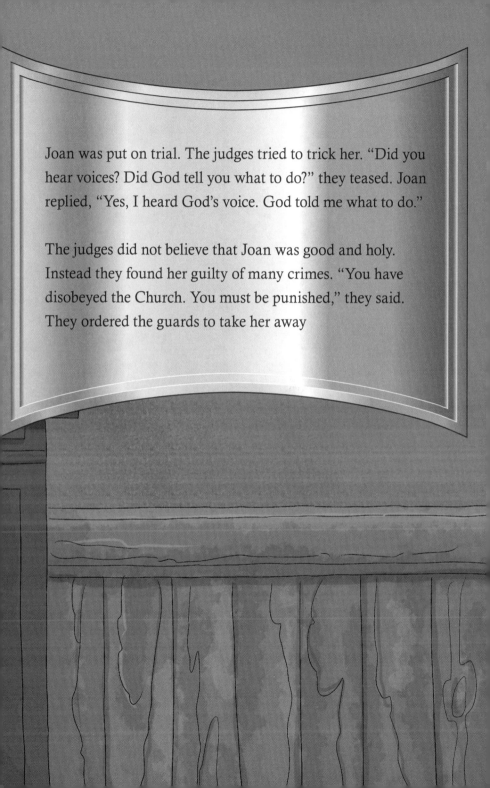

Joan was put on trial. The judges tried to trick her. "Did you hear voices? Did God tell you what to do?" they teased. Joan replied, "Yes, I heard God's voice. God told me what to do."

The judges did not believe that Joan was good and holy. Instead they found her guilty of many crimes. "You have disobeyed the Church. You must be punished," they said. They ordered the guards to take her away

Joan was taken to the marketplace and tied to a pole. Wood was piled at her feet. A fire was started. Someone held up a cross for Joan to see. Joan bowed her head and prayed as the flames reached her. Some people cheered, and others cried.

Years later, a new, fair trial was held. Good people told of Joan's holiness and love of the Church. Joan was not guilty after all. She was innocent!

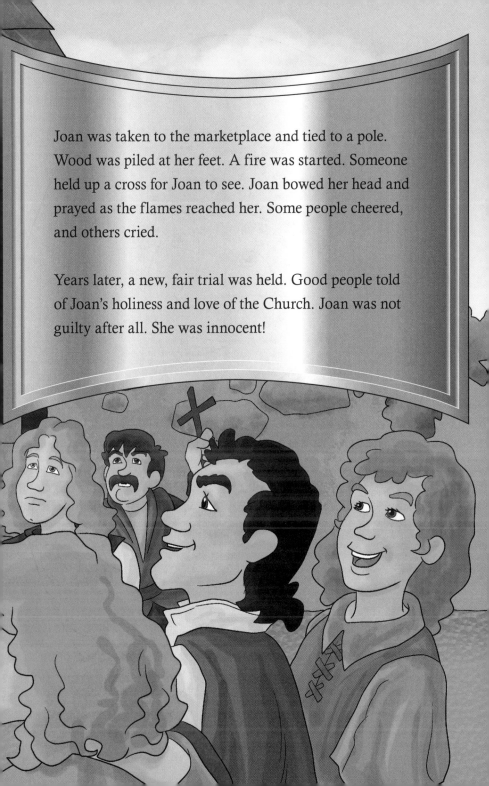

Joan of Arc

Joan of Arc trusted God. She helped to bring peace to France. In 1920, the Catholic Church declared her a saint. Saint Joan of Arc is the patron of soldiers and France.

If God speaks to you today,
What will you do, what will you say?

Dear God.

I love you.

Joan of Arc loved you
with her whole heart.

Help me to be
strong in my faith.

Show me how to be brave
when I am afraid.

Amen.

NEW WORDS (Glossary)

Cathedral: The highest, leading church of a city or area, where the bishop is in charge

Commander: A person who leads an army

Guilty: Responsible for doing something wrong

Innocent: Not guilty of doing something wrong

Orleans: A city in the north-central part of France

Reims: A city in northern France known for its cathedral where French kings were crowned

Trial: The hearing and ruling of a legal case in court

Liguori Publications
saints and me! series
SAINTS FOR COMMUNITIES

Collect the entire set!

JOHN BAPTIST DE LA SALLE
caring Teacher
and mentor

JOAN OF ARC
Brave soldier
for peace

matthew the Apostle
Banker and god's
storyteller

cecilia
singing and sharing
the faith

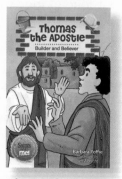

Thomas the Apostle
Builder and Believer

michael
the Archangel
protector of god's people

SAINTS FOR COMMUNITIES
Activity Book

Reproducible activities for all
6 books in the series